A *season* of *sundays*

*Images of the 2014 Gaelic Games year by the Sportsfile team of
photographers, with text by Alan Milton*

An official GAA publication, published by Sportsfile

MATCH DAY TEAM MATES

SUPPORTING THE GAA FOR 24 YEARS

24 Years of Supporting GAA

Once again Carroll's is proud to sponsor *A Season of Sundays* – another demonstration of the company's deep-rooted involvement in Gaelic games as we have sponsored the Offaly county teams for almost a quarter of a century.

Since 1991, the beginning of county shirt sponsorship in the GAA, Carroll's (then Carroll's Meats) has been the only name emblazoned across the Offaly team strips. This makes Carroll's the longest running sponsorship in the GAA.

While Kilkenny and Kerry claimed the 2014 All-Ireland senior hurling and football titles following a thrilling season, as ever a lot of work went on at underage level, and Carroll's played a prominent role in this area.

In 2014 we showed our commitment to developing the abilities of primary school children by running a GAA skills day in O'Connor Park, Tullamore. Two of the outstanding managers in the game – Anthony Daly and Mickey Harte – and some of the leading players – Karl Lacey, Joe Bergin, Liam Rushe and Niall McNamee – were there to share their expertise and skills with the young enthusiasts, giving them a day to remember.

Carroll's is an Irish producer with a proud heritage. We provide over 150 local jobs in our manufacturing plant in Tullamore and support hundreds of jobs indirectly nationwide.

Using traditional family recipes, a Carroll's ham is carefully nurtured, hand-crafted using only the highest quality pork and slow-cooked for a better taste so it truly reflects the pride and passion of the Carroll's family. At Carroll's we take our time getting it right.

We are fully committed to giving something back to the community, and our continued support of Gaelic games and *A Season of Sundays* is proof of that commitment.

We hope you enjoyed a Carroll's ham sandwich on your way to the big matches this year and we are confident that 2015 will also be a season of success.

The Carroll's Team

sportsfile
PUBLISHING

GAA
OFFICIAL PHOTOGRAPHER

Published by:
SPORTSFILE
Patterson House, 14 South Circular Road
Portobello, Dublin 8, Ireland
www.sportsfile.com

Photographs:
Copyright © 2014 Sportsfile

ISBN: 978-1-905468-27-0

Text:
Alan Milton

Editing:
Eddie Longworth

Quotations research:
Seán Creedon

Additional photographs:
Ashleigh Fox, Ray Ryan

Design:
The Design Gang, Tralee

Colour reproduction:
Mark McGrath

Print production:
PB Print Solutions

Case Binding:
Robinson & Mornin Bookbinders Ltd, Belfast

The Sportsfile photographic team:

Barry Cregg

Brendan Moran

Dáire Brennan

David Maher

Diarmuid Greene

Matt Browne

Oliver McVeigh

Pat Murphy

Paul Mohan

Piaras Ó Mídheach

Ramsey Cardy

Ray McManus

Stephen McCarthy

Tomás Greally

Welcome to the club

The scene is the Kerry warm-up area last September, manager Éamonn Fitzmaurice is surrounded by his jubilant players, the clock over his head says 17.43, the Sam Maguire Cup had been lifted 34 minutes earlier.

It was an opportunity to put the achievement of a relatively young Kerry team in perspective and Fitzmaurice, one of the finest coaches in the modern game, was equal to the occasion as he launched into a speech full of emotion and inspiration.

"I just want to say lads, I just want to say to you lads from the bottom of my heart – thanks so much. Ye have no idea lads, ye have no idea the emotion that was in that room [at our meeting] last night, how special and how kind that was, it was unique, it was unique. The fine, massive cup is in front of us. To the boys winning their first All-Ireland – welcome to the club."

Not surprisingly, his words – and especially the punchline – were greeted by loud cheering. The old order had been restored and Sam Maguire was

returning to the Kingdom for the 37th time. It was a stirring speech and reminiscent of the day, in 2010, when I was in the Tipperary hurlers' dressingroom and heard a rousing rendition of *Slievenamon* after they had denied neighbours Kilkenny the five-in-a-row.

Not many outsiders witness such moments, and it's one of the real privileges of my profession as a sports photographer to be invited to such events – on this occasion Éamonn Fitzmaurice had requested my colleague Brendan Moran and me to take a few private photos for the squad in the dressingroom.

But amid all the celebration, back-slapping and jokes about trying Carrauntoohil in training next year, Fitzmaurice touched on one of the unhappy realities of team sport. "This is the sad bit lads," he said, "but this is the last time we'll all be together, with holidays, dos and functions. The entire group won't be together again so enjoy every minute of the next few days and enjoy each other's company."

All in all, it was an electric moment and a privilege to be there.

It was also a terrific season for hurling. The Liam MacCarthy Cup went to Kilkenny in a replay after they and Tipperary had produced one of the greatest exhibitions of hurling ever seen in the drawn match.

I would also like to thank my staff here in the Sportsfile agency. This publication would not be possible without their professionalism and keen eye, and these pages showcase their ability to capture dramatic and spectacular images that will live long in the memory.

Finally, a special word of thanks to Carroll's, the sponsors of this publication. The Carroll's company are long-standing supporters of the GAA in Offaly and *A Season of Sundays*.

Ray McManus

Three whirlwind years as president

Is cúis mhór áthais dom an deis seo a bheith agam fáilte chroíúil a chur roimh an leabhar iontach seo agus muid ag druidim i dtreo dheireadh na bliana arís.

It gives me great satisfaction to again officially welcome on behalf of Cumann Lúthchleas Gael the eagerly-awaited publication of the annual chronicle of excellence that is *A Season of Sundays* – the last time I will be afforded such an opportunity.

In many ways it is hard to believe that it is three years since I first welcomed this wonderful pictorial account of the hurling and football season from start to finish.

In the interim I have seen a lot and the GAA as an organisation has covered a considerable amount of ground.

At most steps along the way a Sportsfile lens has been in close proximity to record moments of importance for the GAA and to preserve for future generations the occasions that matter most.

To say it has been a whirlwind three-year period would be something of an understatement, with visits to every county in Ireland and to many units overseas.

The breadth of the work being undertaken by units of the association – in many instances far beyond the confines of our games – is staggering, and much of it is generated by the goodwill that flows from the games and passages of play captured in this book.

I'm often asked to name the stand-out aspect of being GAA president – particularly from the many young people I come into contact with. And it's appropriate that they should pose the question because it's meeting them, usually in the company of their teachers, that forms the answer.

As someone heavily involved in education, the presence and strength of our games in schools remain on a par with the vibrancy of the club scene – and long may that continue.

This year saw the first concerted effort by the GAA to bring hurling and football to new audiences.

The success of GAAGO and our other broadcasting arrangements outside Ireland have underlined the logic behind the move, and I hope that in future years the excitement generated by the presentation of the photography in this book will extend far beyond our island.

The allure of this book lies in its scope. There is an obvious and justified place for the top-level occasions but, equally, the less celebrated matches command inclusion. Our supporters also grace the season-long voyage, providing the human stories away from the field of play.

The 2013 season was outstanding and many wondered how it could be equalled, but we needn't have worried because 2014 lived up to its billing – and more.

Dublin's rampaging form carried them through the football league and Kilkenny and Tipperary provided another memorable decider in the hurling league. The club championships provided two excellent finals before the intercounty championship fuse was lit.

Thereafter stand-out games came thick and fast. Who will forget the superb meetings of Kilkenny and Galway in the Leinster hurling championship in Tullamore – not least the closing stages of the drawn game?

Or the sea of red and green that greeted the hurlers of Cork and Limerick for the Munster final in the last senior intercounty hurling fixture at Páirc Uí Chaoimh (left) before its redevelopment?

Then fast forward to the All-Ireland series – the heroics of Limerick and Kilkenny in their semi-final deluge; the quality of the three football semi-finals; and an unforgettable hurling final and the need for a replay for the third consecutive year.

The images reproduced in this book are a reminder that we are living through an era to rival any in terms of the quality of our games and the input of our top players.

I would like to thank Ray McManus and his Sportsfile photographers for their unwavering passion for our games, a passion borne out in these pages.

Their diligence and patience are central to their success in capturing award-winning images and, to that end, we owe them a debt of gratitude.

I hope you all derive as much satisfaction from this book as I do, and I wish Ray and his team every success with it, not just this year but for many more to come.

Rath Dé ar an obair.

Liam Ó Néill

LIAM Ó NÉILL
UACHTARÁN CHUMANN LÚTHCHLEAS GAEL

1.

4 Bord na Móna O'Byrne Cup - Páirc Séamus Mhic hEochaidh, Haggardstown, Co Louth
Louth 0-09   DCU 1-15

5 Bord na Móna O'Byrne Cup - O'Kennedy Park, New Ross, Co. Wexford
Wexford 2-13   Laois 0-11

McGrath Cup - Mallow GAA Grounds, Co. Cork
Cork 3-22   Limerick IT 0-07

Bord na Móna O'Byrne Cup - Cusack Park, Mullingar
Westmeath 0-11   Dublin 0-12

2.

3.

4.

(1) Sleepy hollow and trees for goalposts. DCU limber up before an O'Byrne Cup appointment with Louth at Haggardstown

(2) Top, middle or bottom. Tom O'Shea of Geraldine O'Hanrahans arranges the sweet shop merchandise and is togged for the elements

(3) Sign on the dotted line. After his first game in charge of the Cork footballers, Brian Cuthbert signs the jersey of 11-year-old AJ Whelan, from Donoughmore, Co Cork

(4) Meeting your hero. Dublin goalkeeper Stephen Cluxton obliges autograph hunter Will Scahill, aged five from Mullingar, accompanied by his father David. So another generation is hooked

5 Power NI Dr. McKenna Cup - Creggan Kickhams, Randalstown, Co. Antrim
Antrim 0-12   Cavan 3-12

Bord na Móna O'Byrne Cup - Dr. Cullen Park, Carlow
Carlow 2-07   Longford 1-19

FBD League - Tuam Stadium, Tuam
Galway 3-10   Sligo 0-08

Bord na Móna O'Byrne Cup - Páirc Táilteann, Navan
Meath 4-11   DIT 1-14

1.

2.

3

(1) Valley of the squinting windows. Spectators remain indoors
at the Creggan Kickhams clubhouse in Randalstown as Cavan
see off Antrim

(2) Out of the light. In his first match as Longford manager,
Dubliner Jack Sheedy makes his way through the tunnel at
Dr Cullen Park to see his team defeat Carlow

(3) Setting out her stall. Eilish Mannion waits on custom during
Galway's win over Sligo in Tuam

(4) Designer accessory. Offalyman Bernard Allen of DIT places
his gumshield – which reflects his county's colours - behind his
right ear after a defeat to Meath in Navan

4.

8   Bord na Móna O'Byrne Cup - Newtowncashel, Co. Longford
Longford 0-06   Kildare 3-20

Bord na Móna O'Byrne Cup - Parnell Park, Dublin
Dublin 2-06   Louth 0-08

1.   2.

(1) Castle in the air. The box office in Newtowncashel, Longford, looming like a lighthouse in the night as two ticket sellers await patrons

(2) Strength in depth. Daniel Watson raises a green flag for Dublin, slotting the ball past Louth goalkeeper Shane McCoy. Injury and stiff competition combine to limit Watson's involvement thereafter

2.

(1) Messiah in the mist. Fermanagh turn to Down All-Ireland winning manager Pete McGrath, who grapples with the bainisteoir's bib ahead of his first outing – a home date with the Ranch

(2) January lives up to its chilly reputation. Offaly's Eoin Carroll emerges with the ball in an early-season Midlands tussle against Laois

12 Bord na Móna O'Byrne Cup - Parnell Park, Dublin
Dublin 0-16   DCU 3-08

FBD League - Páirc Uí Chonghaile, Collooney, Co. Sligo
Sligo 1-08   GMIT 0-08

FBD League - Connacht GAA Centre of Excellence, Bekan, Co. Mayo
Mayo 2-08   IT Sligo 1-11

1.

2.

(1) Tote-like scrutiny. Seán McNicholas is watched closely as he confirms entry fees at Parnell Park ahead of Dublin's home date with DCU

(2) Owenmore Gaels' Robert Walsh tends to protocol and raises the Galway colours before Sligo host GMIT

(3) Grassy knolls in winter. No need for ponchos here. Seasoned campaigners come prepared to see Mayo draw with IT Sligo in Bekan

3.

12 Bord na Móna O'Byrne Cup - Baltinglass GAA Club, Co. Wicklow
Wicklow 2-05 Meath 4-11

Waterford Crystal Cup - WIT GAA Grounds, Carriganore, Co. Waterford
WIT 1-20 UL 2-30

FBD League - Duggan Park, Ballinasloe
Galway 2-06 Leitrim 1-10

Power NI Dr. McKenna Cup - Athletic Grounds, Armagh
Armagh 0-11 Donegal 1-10

18 Bord na Móna Walsh Cup - Páirc Uí Suiocháin, Gorey
Wexford 4-21 NUIG 0-08

Bord na Móna Walsh Cup - St. Lachtain's GAA Club, Freshford, Co. Kilkenny
Kilkenny 5-23 DIT 1-09

2.

1. 3.

4.

(1) Hawkeye eile. Wicklow County Board president and long-standing journalist Peter Keogh watches Meath beat Wicklow in Baltinglass

(2) Marooned. Waterford IT's Shane O'Sullivan is cut adrift by the UL cavalry

(3) A Lilywhite marooned? Galway's new recruit, Kildare man James Kavanagh, discovers that the January weather doesn't differ west of the Shannon. Leitrim's Emlyn Mulligan also feels the chill

(4) No way out. Donegal's Michael Murphy is surrounded by men in orange – Kieran Toner, Charlie Vernon, Andy Mallon, James Lavery, Finian Moriarty and Ciarán Rafferty – in an early win over Armagh

5.

6.

(5) Shall we? Cormac Devanney of NUIG assumes a waltz-like pose with Wexford's PJ Nolan in a battle for possession

(6) Out the gap. Tommy Walsh makes a swift exit as Brian Cody's musings are sought by journalists. One hallmark of Kilkenny's season would be a turnover in starting personnel

2.

(1) Gladiators. Sticks at the ready, Offaly prepare to emerge for action as Mick Dunne, from Ballinagar, unlocks the gates at O'Connor Park before their duel with Galway

(2) Seasaigí. On the field and in the Healy Park stand all present pay due deference to Amhrán na bhFiann

19 Waterford Crystal Cup - O'Garney Park, Sixmilebridge, Co. Clare
Clare 1-14   Limerick 0-11

McGrath Cup Final - Mallow GAA Grounds, Co. Cork
Cork 1-11   Kerry 0-10

Bord na Móna O'Byrne Cup - St. Conleth's Park, Newbridge
Kildare 5-17   UCD 2-11

1.

2.

3.

(1) Now you see him, later you won't. Limerick joint-managers Donal O'Grady, right, and TJ Ryan survey the Sixmilebridge scene during a Waterford Crystal Cup reversal to Clare. Before league's end the 'joint' prefix will be dropped as O'Grady steps away

(2) Cup-carrying caddie. Alan O'Sullivan, son of Cork selector Ciarán, examines the McGrath Cup after the county's success over Kerry in the final at Mallow

(3) Another case of here today but gone tomorrow. Kerry stalwart Paul Galvin offloads beyond John Hayes of Cork but 13 days later his brother-in-law and manager, Éamonn Fitzmaurice, would announce that Galvin's illustrious career was at an end

(4) Die hard. A lone supporter, with a bleak January skyscape all to himself, sees Kildare hand UCD a lesson with a five-goal salvo

4.

" Welcome to the big league TJ **"**

Davy Fitzgerald reacts to Limerick manager TJ Ryan
who questioned the legality of Clare's tackling in the
Waterford Crystal Cup

21 Bord na Móna Walsh Cup - Parnell Park, Dublin
Dublin 2-20   UCD 2-15

26 Waterford Crystal Cup - O'Garney Park, Sixmilebridge, Co. Clare
Clare 2-28   UCC 1-04

Bord na Móna Walsh Cup - St. Lachtain's GAA Club, Freshford, Co. Kilkenny
Kilkenny 1-24   Galway 0-15

Bord na Móna O'Byrne Cup Final - St. Conleth's Park, Newbridge
Kildare 1-10   Meath 0-09

2.

3.

4.

(1) Come up. UCD and Dublin hurlers jostle for an embedded sliotar in the county team's win in the Walsh Cup encounter at Parnell Park

(2-3) At the start or at the end but ever obliging. Shane O'Donnell's adjustment to celebrity status continues with requests from young female fans before Clare's meeting with UCC. Meanwhile, dab hand Henry Shefflin waits until after his county's win over Galway in Freshford. Included in the throng is 70-year-old Tom Hayes

(4) The start of something big or more of the same? Too early to say is the verdict. Kildare annex another O'Byrne Cup at St Conleth's Park and Eoghan O'Flaherty does the honours

26 FBD League - Páirc Seán Mac Diarmada, Carrick-on-Shannon
Leitrim 2-05   Roscommon 1-07

Bord na Móna Walsh Cup - St. Lachtain's GAA Club, Freshford, Co. Kilkenny
Kilkenny 1-24   Galway 0-15

❝ I would swop this win for two points against Antrim next weekend. That's where our priorities lie. It's great to win the FBD again, but the league is where our focus is **❞**

Leitrim captain Emlyn Mulligan is in no doubt about where his team's priorities lie

1.

2.

(1) Enjoying it when it comes along. Leitrim again show early-season promise to fend off the challenge of Roscommon with FBD League silverware at stake

(2) Grasping at straws. Freshford officials John Fitzpatrick, club chairman John Kennedy and Paddy Buttler use car headlights to help them remove straw from the parking area at their ground

1 Bord na Móna Walsh Cup Final - Croke Park, Dublin
Kilkenny 0-24   Dublin 1-17

Allianz National Football League - Croke Park, Dublin
Dublin 2-08   Kerry 1-10

2 Allianz National Football League - Páirc Uí Rinn, Cork
Cork 0-18   Westmeath 0-10

Allianz National Football League - County Grounds, Aughrim, Co. Wicklow
Wicklow 3-13   London 1-08

2.

1.

3.

(1) Millimetres in a game of inches. A Kilkenny hurler places the sliotar before taking a free in the Walsh Cup final win over Dublin at Croke Park

(2) Kilkenny captain David Langton receives the Walsh Cup silverware as a familiar season-long trend is set in motion

(3) I get by with a little help. Sideline official Liam Devenney assists Kerry's Donnchadh Walsh by tying his bootlace in the county's narrow league defeat to Dublin

(4) It all starts somewhere. Cork manager Brian Cuthbert, putting his stamp on the squad, addresses the players before their home league win over Westmeath

(5) Caged in. Wicklow manager Harry Murphy cuts a solitary figure as he clutches his match programme

4.

5.

2   2013 Ulster GAA Hurling Senior Championship Final - Celtic Park, Derry
Antrim 4-20 Down 1-17

7   Waterford Crystal Cup Final - Gaelic Grounds, Limerick
Tipperary 4-22 Clare 3-11

8   AIB GAA Hurling All-Ireland Senior Club Championship Semi-Final - Semple Stadium, Thurles
Portumna 1-15 Na Piarsaigh 1-11

9   Allianz National Football League - Páirc Uí Rinn, Cork
Cork 0-16 Kildare 1-12

  Allianz National Football League - Pearse Stadium, Salthill
Galway 0-12 Donegal 1-16

(1) Better late than never. Antrim captain Neil McManus puts his best foot forward with the Liam Harvey Cup after the delayed staging of the 2013 Ulster hurling final

(2) Crystal clear. Tipperary captain James Woodlock collects the Waterford Crystal trophy after his team finish with something to spare over Clare

(3) Summer sun or winter rain, it doesn't matter. Joe Canning of Portumna keeps his eyes on the sliotar despite the challenge posed by William O'Donoghue of Na Piarsaigh and the downpour. Portumna advance

1.

2.

3.

(4) Touch tight, and it's still spilling rain. Gary White of Kildare gets little wriggle room from Cork's Ruairí Deane in his team's away defeat

(5) Patience is a virtue. Colm McFadden jokes with Galway goalkeeper Manus Breathnach while a young autograph hunter waits for the Donegal man to sign a programme in Salthill

" Forwards are taking on their men more and backs are afraid to over-commit. They just don't want to take the risk of that black card, it's definitely a factor "

Kildare manager Jason Ryan feels the introduction of the black card encourages more attacking football

4.

5.

9 Allianz National Football League - Healy Park, Omagh
Tyrone 2-15   Mayo 0-16

Allianz National Football League - Fitzgerald Stadium, Killarney
Kerry 0-14   Derry 0-16

Allianz National Football League - Kiltoom, Co. Roscommon
Roscommon 1-16   Wexford 1-09

(1) Eyes locked on. Mayo full back Ger Cafferkey and Tyrone's Darren McCurry, both with aspirations of long summers, get in close in Omagh league action

(2) On the move. Kerry supporter Fionnán Cogan, aged three, takes a look around as Derry beat Kerry in Killarney

(3) Colour coded. The compulsory new gumshields are on full view as Donie Shine rises highest and claims the ball above his Roscommon team-mate Kevin Higgins and Wexford's Brian Malone and James Breen

1.

2.

3.

" It's a seven-hour journey back to Derry, but it will be a nice, relaxed bus "

Manager Brian McIver after Derry's first win over Kerry in Killarney since 1993

1.

1. Sharp focus, out of focus. The Tipperary team photograph is captured on a smartphone at Semple Stadium. The hosts see off Waterford's challenge

2. Just another fan? Unhindered and hooded, All-Ireland winning manager Davy Fitzgerald walks the Cusack Park concourse before his team's home league win over Kilkenny

" I am genuinely shocked. I didn't think they would have that much in the tank. But maybe the trimming we got against Waterford in the Crystal Cup hurt my players "

A pleased Clare manager Davy Fitzgerald after his team's one-point win over Kilkenny

2.

16 Allianz National Hurling League - O'Connor Park, Tullamore
Offaly 2-14   Laois 1-19

Allianz National Hurling League - Pearse Stadium, Salthill
Galway 0-28   Dublin 1-12

22 Allianz National Hurling League - O'Moore Park, Portlaoise
Laois 0-07   Cork 0-14

23 Allianz National Hurling League - Nowlan Park, Kilkenny
Kilkenny 5-20   Tipperary 5-14

1.

2.

3.

(1) 'Say that again.' Brian Whelahan converses by phone before Laois spring a surprise against Offaly in the league, one of many setbacks for the former All Star in a difficult first season as county manager

(2) New campaign, similar challenges. Galway manager Anthony Cunningham and Anthony Daly, his Dublin counterpart, shake hands in Salthill before a comfortable win for the home team

(3) Putting the boot in. An untied lace and Stephen McDonnell loses his right boot in a tussle with Patrick Whelan. Cork prevail in Portlaoise but not before a significant test

(4) No roof over their heads. The skeletal remains of the Nowlan Park stand are testimony to the damage wreaked by the February storms, as Brendan Maher of Tipperary and host captain Lester Ryan shake hands alongside referee Diarmuid Kirwan

" It was a great game, but not great to concede five goals. We were open for the goals as we were trying a few different things; some came off, some didn't "

Tipperary manager Eamon O'Shea muses on the 10-goal thriller at Nowlan Park

23 Allianz National Hurling League - Walsh Park, Waterford
Waterford 0-22 Galway 1-13

M Donnelly Football Interprovincial Championship Final - Tuam Stadium, Tuam
Connacht 2-19 Ulster 1-07

Allianz National Hurling League - Parnell Park, Dublin
Dublin 2-17 Clare 0-17

Allianz National Hurling League - Gaelic Grounds, Limerick
Limerick 3-26 Antrim 0-12

2.

3.

4.

(1) Into the light. The silhouetted figure of Galway captain David Burke appears to hover freely suspended as he makes his way to the Walsh Park pitch for a league clash against Waterford

(2) History making witnessed by few. Mayo's Keith Higgins is interviewed by Michael Gallagher after he had become the first Connacht man to claim interprovincial honours in both codes, courtesy of the footballers' win over Ulster in Tuam

(3) Job done, put it there. Dublin team doctor Dr Chris Thompson greets Alan McCrabbe as he leaves the field towards the end of the Dubs' impressive victory over Clare

(4) Mixed signals from Limerick's joint managers. Donal O'Grady uses two fingers and TJ Ryan one to get their point across in the home league win over Antrim. O'Grady resigned his position two months later

1.

2.

❝ We struggled to score in the second half again.
It is becoming a pattern and a worrying pattern ❞

A concerned Éamonn Fitzmaurice after Kerry's defeat to Mayo in Castlebar

(1) Best foot forward. Armagh's Oisín McKeever prepares for lift-off against Meath at Páirc Tailteann

(2) Rough terrain is nothing new to Mayo football. The county's players go off road en route to the warm-up facility in Castlebar

2 Allianz National Football League - O'Donnell Park, Letterkenny
Donegal 2-11   Monaghan 0-10

8 Allianz National Football League - Croke Park, Dublin
Dublin 1-22   Kildare 1-12

Allianz National Football League - Athletic Grounds, Armagh
Armagh 2-18   Laois 1-12

1.

2.

(1) Heightened awareness. Donegal's analytical requirements see members of their backroom team take an elevated position for the Letterkenny league assignment with Monaghan

(2) Dublin's Davy Byrne goes full tilt to claim possession against Kildare's Paul Cribbin. The men in blue claim two points in emphatic fashion

(3) Space at a premium. Gary Walsh of Laois pulls the trigger in a crowded Armagh goalmouth but his attempt is saved by goalkeeper Philip McAvoy

9 Allianz National Football League - Cusack Park, Mullingar
Westmeath 3-09   Mayo 2-17

Allianz National Hurling League - Nowlan Park, Kilkenny
Kilkenny 2-16   Galway 1-16

1.

2.

(1) Played seven, lost seven. In a scene that typified Westmeath's brief stay in Division One of the league, Gavin Hoey is engulfed by Mayo men in Mullingar – Seamus O'Shea, Donal Vaughan, Lee Keegan, David Drake, Aidan O'Shea and Colm Boyle

(2) The Cats are generally one step ahead of the rest. Duties completed and Kilkenny victorious over Galway, Nowlan Park groundsman Timmy Grogan has a spring in his step as he carries the ladder and the sign across the field

15 Allianz National Football League - Athletic Grounds, Armagh
Armagh 0-10   Monaghan 1-17

16 Allianz National Football League - Elverys MacHale Park, Castlebar
Mayo 4-12   Cork 2-14

Allianz National Football League - Celtic Park, Derry
Derry 1-16   Dublin 0-13

1.

(1) At full stretch. Stefan Forker of Armagh has his jersey tested by Monaghan's Fintan Kelly

(2) Knowing glances. The home supporters in Castlebar realise that Mayo manager James Horan is taking up a position among them in the stand for the second half of the win over Cork

(3) Airborne. Michael Darragh Macauley surges forward against Benny Heron and Kevin Johnston of Derry. The Dubs get their wings clipped by the Foyle

2.

3.

1.

2.

MARCH '14

17 AIB GAA Hurling All-Ireland Senior Club Championship Final - Croke Park, Dublin
Portumna 0-19   Mount Leinster Rangers 0-11

AIB GAA Football All-Ireland Senior Club Championship Final - Croke Park, Dublin
St. Vincent's 4-12   Castlebar Mitchels 2-11

3.

4.

5.

(1) Hanging in the balance. Portumna's Joe Canning appears to hold the advantage in this aerial duel with Páraig Nolan of Mount Leinster Rangers

(2) The Colgate smile says it all. Captain Ollie Canning lifts the Tommy Moore Cup after Portumna's fourth All-Ireland club hurling final success

(3) Patrick Durcan of Castlebar Mitchels holds off the challenge of St Vincent's Tomás Quinn in the All-Ireland club football final

(4) Numero uno - officially. Kevin Bonnie assumes a celebratory pose understood in all languages and cultures and is held aloft by Luke Bree after St Vincent's All-Ireland club victory

(5) Hats off to Vinnies. The Andy Merrigan Cup loses its lid as team captain Ger Brennan declares party time in Marino

❝ Maybe when I am manager Tommy Conroy's young age I will be able to look back with fond memories on what we have achieved. As a young player you tend to live in the present and you don't fully understand the impact of your achievements **❞**

St Vincent's captain Ger Brennan responding to questions on what victory in the All-Ireland club final meant to him

49

29 Allianz National Football League - Croke Park, Dublin
Dublin 3-14   Mayo 2-17

30 Allianz National Football League - Cusack Park, Mullingar
Westmeath 0-13   Kerry 2-15

Allianz National Hurling League Quarter-Final - Gaelic Grounds, Limerick
Limerick 1-12   Galway 1-20

Allianz National Hurling League Relegation Play-Off - Walsh Park, Waterford
Waterford 1-17   Dublin 4-13

Allianz National Hurling League Quarter-Final - Semple Stadium, Thurles
Tipperary 3-25   Cork 4-19

Allianz National Hurling League Quarter-Final - O'Moore Park, Portlaoise
Laois 2-19   Clare 2-23

2.

1.

3.

4.

(1) Presidential endorsement. The president of the GAA, Liam Ó Néill, applauds Kerry's Division 2A hurling league final success as captain John Egan hoists silverware

(2) A family affair. Donegal's Jamesie Donnelly toasts the county's Division 3A league final win over Roscommon at Markievicz Park with daughter Ella, three, and son James, two months

(3) 'Smile, you're on camera.' The injured Colm Cooper conjures up a wry smile for the cameras in Tralee on a day when his absence from the Kerry team is particularly pronounced, Cork winning by 10 points

(4) Watching brief. Taoiseach Enda Kenny looks on intently in Castlebar as his native Mayo beat Derry

(5) Hurlers but very few hurleys. Tyrone gather for the group photo after their Division 3B title success

(6) Striding purposefully. The familiar figure of Jim McGuinness mans the line at the Athletic Grounds as Donegal beat Armagh. It will be another big year for the Celtic FC employee

6.

" We got a bit of momentum and they found it hard to come back **"**

Manager Jim Gavin plays down Dublin's easy win over Derry in the league final

3 Cadbury GAA Football All-Ireland U-21 Championship Final - O'Connor Park, Tullamore
Dublin 1-21   Roscommon 3-06

4 Allianz National Hurling League Division 1 Final - Semple Stadium, Thurles
Kilkenny 2-25   Tipperary 1-27

(1) No one is safe from the selfie craze. The Dublin under-21 footballers pose for the camera after a surprisingly facile win over Roscommon in the final in Tullamore

(2) Well done. Tipperary duo Noel McGrath and Pádraic Maher, showered and changed, congratulate Kilkenny captain Lester Ryan, who is still on the pitch 40 minutes after their league final win

1.   2.

❝ Hurling is the game that just keeps on giving ❞

Former Tipp star turned analyst, Nicky English, after another terrific tussle between his native county and Kilkenny

4   Connacht GAA Football Senior Championship - Gaelic Park, Bronx, New York
New York 0-08   Mayo 4-18

17   Leinster GAA Football Senior Championship - Cusack Park, Mullingar
Westmeath 1-09   Louth 1-14

1.

2.

(1) The train, the Stars and Stripes and the green scoreboard, it has to be the Bronx.
Meanwhile, Mayo captain Andy Moran keeps his team-mates waiting for the team
photo before their clash with New York

(2) A leaf from the Babas' book. Louth players warm up in their club jerseys in a
gesture that is widely noted, particularly as they went on to beat hosts Westmeath

the **DNA** of the **GAA**

An army marches on its stomach

The San Siro it ain't. But therein lies the allure.

It's the simple things in life that matter as Eugene Killen, left, and Eddie Caughey, both from Newcastle, Co Down, enjoy a sandwich and a cup of tea ahead of the game.

Its simplicity, its tradition, its earthy relevance all combine to fuel lifelong engagement, fulfilment and meaning as so many other strands of life continue to evolve and change.

It's a scene repeated in countless locations up and down the island - and indeed further afield – by those who love Gaelic football and hurling.

The colours - if any are visible - and accents may differ but the connection remains the same. It is non-negotiable and of the cradle-to-the-grave variety.

It's a constant, a tradition rooted in a subconscious, generational hand-down. Father taking daughter to the local field; mother taking son to a county ground for the first time.

Colours not chosen but conferred and confirmed.

More senior generations may not appreciate it but their bond to the games and the GAA as an organisation inspires those coming behind, serving as a template, hinting at how it has always been.

Their dedication and commitment to, and fascination in, the games become the norm. It's in the social fabric of the island.

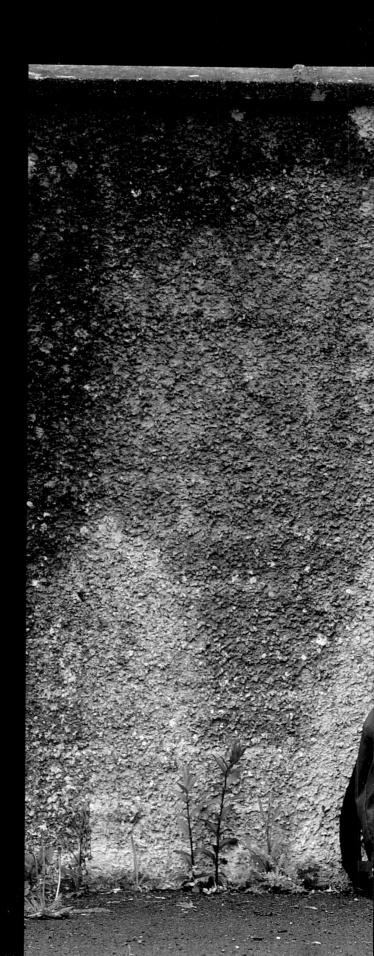

18 Ulster GAA Football Senior Championship - Healy Park, Omagh
Tyrone 2-11 Down 3-08

Leinster GAA Hurling Senior Championship Qualifier Group - Dr. Cullen Park, Carlow
Carlow 0-14 Westmeath 1-09

Leinster GAA Football Senior Championship - Pearse Park, Longford
Longford 0-19 Offaly 0-15

Connacht GAA Football Senior Championship - Dr. Hyde Park, Roscommon
Roscommon 1-18 Leitrim 0-13

24 Leinster GAA Hurling Senior Championship Qualifier Group - Cusack Park, Mullingar
Westmeath 2-12 London 1-12

Ulster GAA Football Senior Championship Replay - Páirc Esler, Newry
Down 0-12 Tyrone 3-11

2.

1.

3.

4.

(1) Up and running. Tyrone and Down collide in an early championship blockbuster in Omagh. It's honours even in the first encounter as Mattie Donnelly and Ambrose Rogers compete

(2) Pushing upwards. Westmeath hurling manager Brian Hanley shakes the hand of his Carlow counterpart John Meyler. In a battle between two counties working for the breakthrough, it's Carlow who edge this encounter

(3) The sweet sound of the final whistle… when you're ahead. Longford manager Jack Sheedy savours the moment

(4) Meet you halfway. Roscommon manager John Evans offers the hand of friendship to his Leitrim counterpart Seán Hagan. Roscommon's early-season form extends to the opening stages of the championship

(5) Can we rewind that last passage of play? London's Keith Killilea reacts to a missed chance during his team's narrow defeat at the hands of Westmeath in Mullingar

(6) The one that got away. Down midfielder Kevin McKernan rues his team's shortcomings in the replay against Tyrone as they bow out of contention in Ulster

5.

6.

2.

(1) High vis unity. Donegal are the latest county to add fluorescent colours to their training attire. Manager Jim McGuinness holds sway before the county's away win over Derry

(2) Antrim hurling manager Kevin Ryan checks the programme line-ups as he prepares for the Leinster championship joust against Laois in O'Moore Park. However, Ryan leaves Portlaoise with a spring in his step

25 Munster GAA Hurling Senior Championship - Semple Stadium, Thurles
Waterford 1-21   Cork 1-21

Connacht GAA Football Senior Championship - Emerald Park, Ruislip, London
London 0-07   Galway 3-17

31 Munster GAA Football Senior Championship - Gaelic Grounds, Limerick
Limerick 1-11   Tipperary 2-14

1.

(1) Flashing before their eyes. Waterford's hurlers watch the photographers click into action as they get the early formalities out of the way before their draw against Cork in Thurles

(2) 'When are you coming back to us?' Gary O'Donnell, right, greets fellow Galwayman Damien Dunleavy, now wearing the green of London. Galway prevail and snuff out the dream of another Connacht adventure for the Exiles

(3) Sun on their backs and shadows out in front. Limerick's Ian Ryan tries to get away from Tipperary's Steven O'Brien

1   Ulster GAA Football Senior Championship - Brewster Park, Enniskillen
Fermanagh 3-13   Antrim 2-18

Munster GAA Hurling Senior Championship - Semple Stadium, Thurles
Tipperary 2-16   Limerick 2-18

(1) Saffron delight. Kevin Niblock and Seán McVeigh celebrate Antrim's win over Fermanagh in Enniskillen. The reaction of Ruairí Corrigan and Barry Owens reveals the flipside of the tale

(2) A gazelle-like entrance from Shane Dowling is indicative of the spring Limerick bring to the first defence of their Munster crown against Tipperary at Semple Stadium

1.

2.

" I have defended Tipperary's hurlers in the past, but I honestly don't think you can defend the performance they delivered against Limerick "

Former Waterford hurler turned analyst, John Mullane, despairs for the Premier County

1   Leinster GAA Hurling Senior Championship - O'Moore Park, Portlaoise
Laois 0-23   Galway 1-22

7   Leinster GAA Hurling Senior Championship - Nowlan Park, Kilkenny
Kilkenny 5-32   Offaly 1-18

Munster GAA Football Senior Championship - Cusack Park, Ennis
Clare 2-08   Waterford 2-08

1.

2.

" This wasn't a pretty day for Offaly hurling. It's going to take a lot of soul-searching, a lot of hard work. All we can do is look to the future, to the qualifiers. But that's only a small stepping stone **"**

Offaly forward Brian Carroll after his side's heavy defeat to Kilkenny

3.

(1) A class act in a crowded area. It's late in the game and Galway star Joe Canning is deep in the trenches, helping his defenders withstand another Laois onslaught

(2) The sky is the limit – cliched or true? A Sky Sports camera man is in position at Nowlan Park for the station's first live GAA broadcast, Kilkenny's filleting of Offaly

(3) Waterford's Thomas O'Gorman shows soft hands in taking possession ahead of Martin O'Leary of Clare

7 Lory Meagher Cup Final - Croke Park, Dublin
Longford 3-18   Fermanagh 3-16

Nicky Rackard Cup Final - Croke Park, Dublin
Tyrone 1-17   Fingal 1-16

Christy Ring Cup Final - Croke Park, Dublin
Kildare 4-18   Kerry 2-22

2.

3.

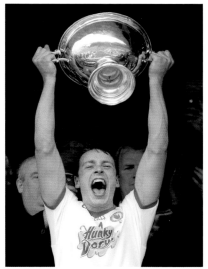

4.

1)   She doesn't appreciate it now but… Longford's Conor Egan celebrates with his eight-month-old daughter Elayna, the Lory Meagher Cup and his team-mates following the county's win over Fermanagh in the final

2)   Mascots aplenty. The Kildare hurlers mark their surprise Christy Ring Cup final success over Kerry with a Croke Park team photo

3)   Up she goes. Tyrone hurling captain Damien Casey does the honours with gusto after the county's one-point Nicky Rackard Cup win over Fingal

4)   Longford hurling captain Martin Coyle sports a satisfied grin after receiving the Lory Meagher Cup

8   Leinster GAA Football Senior Championship - Croke Park, Dublin
Kildare 1-22   Louth 1-07

Leinster GAA Football Senior Championship - Croke Park, Dublin
Dublin 2-21   Laois 0-16

Ulster GAA Football Senior Championship - Athletic Grounds, Armagh
Armagh 1-12   Cavan 0-09

Connacht GAA Football Senior Championship - Dr. Hyde Park, Roscommon
Roscommon 1-09   Mayo 0-13

1.

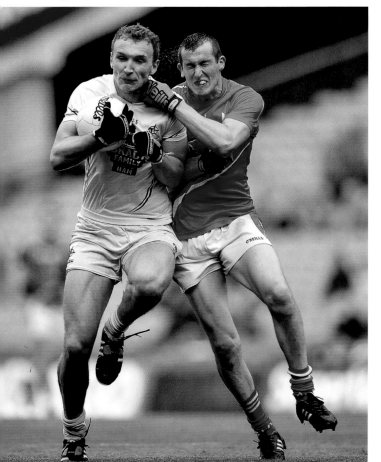

2.

3.

❝ Roscommon had the momentum, the crowd and the wind. They had everything with them. It would have been easy to lie down but the character and resolve our guys showed today was excellent **❞**

Mayo manager James Horan is happy with the determination shown by his side during their one-point win over Roscommon at Dr Hyde Park

4.

(1) Braced for contact. Tommy Moolick holds on tightly to possession as the hit arrives from Louth's Dessie Finnegan. The Lilywhites score a surprisingly easy win

(2) Warming up – literally. The Laois footballers jump as they go through their warm-up routine before the Leinster joust with Dublin. Despite leading at the interval Laois's challenge eventually fades

(3) We're coming in the back way. Armagh manager Paul Grimley and his panel take an alternative route into the Athletic Grounds for their meeting with Cavan. A pre-match melee over the position of county flags for the parade dominates the post-match commentary

(4) It's not that bad. Mayo defender Lee Keegan commiserates with a visibly disappointed Finbar Cregg of Roscommon. Mayo sneak home with a point to spare

8 Munster GAA Hurling Senior Championship Replay - Semple Stadium, Thurles
Cork 0-28   Waterford 0-14

14 Leinster GAA Hurling Senior Championship - Wexford Park, Wexford
Wexford 1-14   Dublin 0-22

1.

(1) Here we go again – for the last time? Anthony Nash raises the sliotar in his trademark style of penalty-taking but this time his rocket is thwarted by the bravery of Waterford goalkeeper Stephen O'Keeffe who races from his line to block. A few days later the GAA changed the rule on taking penalties.

(2) 'When I grow up.' Wexford goalkeeper Mark Fanning finds time for a laugh with a young supporter at half-time in the home championship encounter with Dublin

2.

" It's absolutely unbelievable to have come on as a sub.
The reaction from the crowd was great **"**

Cork hurler Paudie O'Sullivan's delight at the reception he received from
both sets of supporters following a year-long lay-off due to injury

29   Leinster GAA Football Senior Championship - Croke Park, Dublin
Dublin 2-25   Wexford 1-12

Ulster GAA Hurling Senior Championship - St Tiernach's Park, Clones
Down 3-28   Derry 5-22

5   GAA Football All-Ireland Senior Championship Round 2A - Semple Stadium, Thurles
Tipperary 2-17   Longford 0-06

Ulster GAA Hurling Senior Championship Replay - Athletic Grounds, Armagh
Down 1-15   Derry 2-19

1.

2.

3.

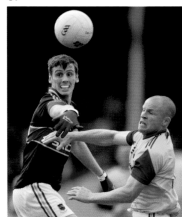

4.

(1) All for one, one for all. Wexford appear full of purpose as they break from the team photo ahead of their assignment with Dublin. When the match begins that sense of purpose quickly evaporates

(2) Dropping the blade. Derry's Paul Cleary prepares to take a sideline cut in his county's Ulster championship meeting with Down

(3) It's a long way down. Tipperary's Conor Sweeney and Dermot Brady of Longford wait for gravity to take over as Longford return to earth with a bang following their great win over Derry

(4) In around the back. Down's Johnny McCusker goes for the unconventional in his attempt to dispossess Tiarnan McCloskey of Derry

5
GAA Football All-Ireland Senior Championship Round 2A - County Grounds, Aughrim, Co. Wicklow
Wicklow 0-10   Sligo 0-12

GAA Hurling All-Ireland Senior Championship Round 1 - Cusack Park, Ennis
Clare 2-25   Wexford 2-25

GAA Football All-Ireland Senior Championship Round 2A - Gaelic Grounds, Limerick
Limerick 3-11   Antrim 0-15

GAA Hurling All-Ireland Senior Championship Round 1 - Semple Stadium, Thurles
Tipperary 3-25   Galway 4-13

1.

2.

(1) Hanging on to stay upright. Brendan Egan loses his footing and appears to bring Wicklow's Dean Healy down with him in Sligo's qualifier victory in Aughrim

(2) Eyes on the prize. Liam Óg McGovern of Wexford leads the way from Clare's Colm Galvin in a dramatic draw in Ennis

(3) The long, unbooted walk. Antrim goalkeeper Patrick Flood cuts a lonely figure heading for the dressingroom after his team's qualifier reversal to Limerick in the Gaelic Grounds

(4) Not letting go. Daithí Burke of Galway tries to escape the clutches of Tipperary duo Patrick Maher and Séamus Callanan. He and Galway fall short

3.

4.

> **❝** The Cork footballers remind me of what Churchill said about Russia, 'It's a riddle, wrapped in a mystery, inside an enigma.' **❞**

Sunday Independent columnist Colm O'Rourke on the Cork footballers *before* their Munster final defeat to Kerry

12
GAA Hurling All-Ireland Senior Championship Round 1 Replay - Wexford Park, Wexford
Wexford 2-25   Clare 2-22

GAA Football All-Ireland Senior Championship Round 3A - Markievicz Park, Sligo
Sligo 0-12   Limerick 0-10

GAA Hurling All-Ireland Senior Championship Round 2 - O'Moore Park, Portlaoise
Tipperary 5-25   Offaly 1-20

GAA Football All-Ireland Senior Championship Round 2B - Kingspan Breffni Park, Cavan
Cavan 0-05   Roscommon 0-16

GAA Football All-Ireland Senior Championship Round 3A - O'Moore Park, Portlaoise
Laois 4-09   Tipperary 3-17

4.

5.

(1) For whom the bell tolls. Clare manager Davy Fitzgerald, reacting to a decision against his team, sees the reigning All-Ireland champions bow out – beaten in extra time in the replay as Wexford's unexpected renaissance continues

(2) Business transaction. Euros are exchanged for an official match programme in Markievicz Park before the qualifier meeting of Sligo and Limerick

(3) Not our day. Seán Cleary's reaction sums up a day to forget for Offaly as Tipperary's season gathers momentum

(4) These guys don't need tickets. The Roscommon footballers, led by Cathal Cregg and Enda Smith, make their way to the main auditorium following their pre-match warm-up outside Kingspan Breffni Park. The ritual works as they account for the hosts with ease

(5) Clenched fists normally equate to satisfaction. It applies in this instance to Conor Sweeney after he scores his second goal in Tipperary's win over Laois

13

GAA Football All-Ireland Senior Championship Round 2B - Páirc Esler, Newry
Down 0-11   Kildare 1-18

GAA Football All-Ireland Senior Championship Round 2B - Healy Park, Omagh
Tyrone 0-10   Armagh 0-13

GAA Football All-Ireland Senior Championship Round 2B - Dr. Cullen Park, Carlow
Carlow 2-13   Clare 4-26

Ulster GAA Hurling Senior Championship Final - Owenbeg, Dungiven, Co. Derry
Derry 2-16   Antrim 2-17

1.

2.

3.

(1) Tuned in. Ciarán McPolin, aged seven, from Mayobridge, Co Down, listens attentively to the musical instructions before Down's defeat to Kildare in Newry

(2) Ready to rock. Armagh's Ciarán McKeever looks totally focused on the job in hand as he leads his team out for their away assignment with Tyrone. The captain's pre-match approach yields the right result

(3) Plant it right there. Carlow manager Anthony Rainbow gets a kiss from his three-year-old daughter Robin following his team's qualifier defeat to Clare

(4) Two Ulster titles in six months. Antrim celebrate their Ulster final win over Derry, retaining the trophy after winning the 2013 title in February

1.

2.

3

❝ The goals were the difference, let's be honest about that ❞

As usual Cork manager Jimmy Barry Murphy is very succinct in his summary of
the Rebels' victory over Limerick in the Munster hurling final

(1) In the nick of time – for Barry Moran that is. The realisation dawns on Galway goalkeeper Manus Breathnach that he is not going to make it, and Mayo have goal number three in the Connacht final

(2) One down, a bigger one on the horizon. Mayo captain Andy Moran raises the Nestor Cup and the Connacht champions are officially on the All-Ireland series circuit again

(3) A detached observer? Limerick manager TJ Ryan can't hide his anguish during the second half of his team's dethroning as Munster champions by Cork

(4) Over the top? Limerick's Graeme Mulcahy goes to ground with Shane O'Neill and Mark Ellis of Cork in close proximity

13 Munster GAA Hurling Senior Championship Final - Páirc Uí Chaoimh, Cork
Cork 2-24   Limerick 0-24

1.

2.

(1) Portrait perfect. Cork's Lorcán McLoughlin clears his lines despite an attempted block by Graeme Mulcahy on a picturesque last day at the current Páirc Uí Chaoimh

(2) The sanctuary of a winning dressingroom. The Cork hurlers pose in the afterglow of a Munster final success over Limerick

1.

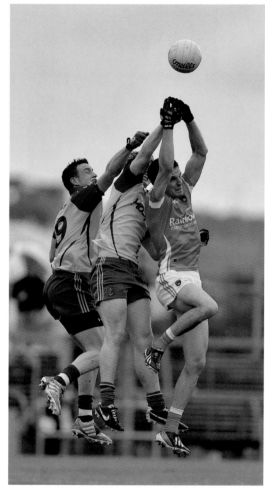

2.

3.

" It's fantastic. People in Wexford have been looking for a team to follow for a long time and they have a team now "

Wexford manager Liam Dunne after their win over Waterford at Nowlan Park set up an All-Ireland quarter-final meeting with Limerick

19 GAA Football All-Ireland Senior Championship Round 3B - Dr. Hyde Park, Roscommon
Roscommon 1-12 Armagh 1-17

GAA Hurling All-Ireland Senior Championship Round 2 - Nowlan Park, Kilkenny
Wexford 3-15 Waterford 2-15

GAA Football All-Ireland Senior Championship, Round 3B - Cusack Park, Ennis
Clare 0-12 Kildare 0-13

20 Leinster GAA Football Senior Championship Final - Croke Park, Dublin
Dublin 3-20 Meath 1-10

4.

5.

(1) Put your fist through it. Roscommon's Kevin Higgins opts for the closed fist option as his team-mate David Keenan and Armagh's Stephen Harold compete in an aerial duel. Armagh advance and gather more momentum

(2) Two-dimensional? Not this summer. Wexford supporters raise a cardboard cut-out of hurling team manager Liam Dunne in familiar pose. The Wexford bandwagon rolls on with a one-goal win over Waterford in Nowlan Park

(3) Defeat is often harder to digest when the margin is narrow. It's as slender as it can possibly be against Kildare and the disappointment of Clare duo Jamie Malone and Stephen Collins tells you all you need to know

(4) Queueing up – literally. Bernard and Alan Brogan compete to see which of them will pull on the loose ball first as the Dubs bag a goal in the Leinster final win over Meath

(5) Five from five. Dublin captain Stephen Cluxton is making a habit of this as he receives the Delaney Cup. It's back-to-back National League and Leinster wins for Dublin and it sets up the possibility of a bigger back-to-back success

20 Ulster GAA Football Senior Championship Final - St. Tiernach's Park, Clones
Donegal 0-15 Monaghan 1-09

26 GAA Football All-Ireland Senior Championship Round 4A - O'Connor Park, Tullamore
Galway 4-17 Tipperary 4-12

GAA Football All-Ireland Senior Championship Round 4A - O'Connor Park, Tullamore
Cork 0-21 Sligo 1-11

1.

2.

3

❝ It was a physical game, but we dealt with the physicality better. We were smarter and more intelligent on the ball than we were last year. We made it easy for Monaghan last year **❞**

Donegal manager Jim McGuinness following the win over Monaghan in the Ulster final in Clones

4.

(1) Halting his gallop. Drew Wylie and Dermot Malone attempt to delay Colm McFadden as Donegal return to Clones and avenge the Ulster final defeat of 12 months earlier to the same opposition

(2) The Anglo-Celt Cup is back in the north west and neither Donegal nor their manager Jim McGuinness attempt to hide their satisfaction with the feat following a testing 2013

(3) Tipperary football manager Peter Creedon barely has time to check his watch as the scores come thick and fast in an entertaining shootout with Galway. But it's the Westerners who have more on the board at the end

(4) Inches and sinews. James Loughrey of Cork and Sligo's David Kelly compete for possession in the qualifier in Tullamore. The Connacht men fail to test the beaten Munster finalists

27 GAA Hurling All-Ireland Senior Championship Quarter-Final - Semple Stadium, Thurles
Limerick 4-26 Wexford 1-11

GAA Hurling All-Ireland Senior Championship Quarter-Final - Semple Stadium, Thurles
Tipperary 2-23 Dublin 0-16

2.

(1) Is it any better through one eye? Eight-year-old Wexford supporter Jimmy Connors surveys the wreckage as his team implode against Limerick in the quarter-final at Semple Stadium

(2) One of those days. The frustration and disappointment bubble to the surface for Dublin manager Anthony Daly towards the end of their championship exit at the hands of Tipperary in Thurles. He may have had an inkling at the time but in due course his long and successful association with Dublin hurling would come to an end with this game

1.

(1) Straying into a tangerine web. Meath's Damien Carroll is encircled by Mark Shields, Stefan Campbell, Stephen Harold and Andy Mallon as Armagh claim another championship win

(2) Floodlights – literally. Monaghan and Kildare bear the brunt of the inclement August weather as the heavens open. Monaghan fare best in the rain

" We are delighted to have got the victory. We knew the history books were against us in that we hadn't won a championship match at Croke Park in 84 years. In extra-time, I thought we got stronger and that's when we really showed the hunger **"**

A thoroughly relieved Monaghan manager Malachy O'Rourke after his team ended their long wait for a championship win at headquarters

2 GAA Football All-Ireland Senior Championship Round 4B - Croke Park, Dublin
Monaghan 2-16   Kildare 2-14

Growing in the dark. The final whistle has long since sounded
and the last person to leave has turned out almost all of the lights.
One patch of the Croke Park pitch receives special overnight
attention in an effort to encourage growth

3 GAA Football All-Ireland Senior Championship Quarter-Final - Croke Park, Dublin
Kerry 1-20   Galway 2-10

GAA Football All-Ireland Senior Championship Quarter-Final - Croke Park, Dublin
Mayo 1-19   Cork 2-15

1.

(1) Kerry's new dangerman James O'Donoghue celebrates his goal against Galway, and his burgeoning reputation gains new admirers

(2) Holding the line. Mayo defenders man their goalline in an effort to thwart a late Cork comeback in their quarter-final. They succeed and Cork go out

" Paul Geaney and myself are not the biggest threat in the Kerry team. We create chances, but we go through spells where we need to improve and I'm sure our manager Éamonn Fitzmaurice will be telling us all about that. We have a bit of work to do "

James O'Donoghue explains how the Kerry forward line is adapting as they progress in the championship

9 GAA Football All-Ireland Senior Championship Quarter-Final - Croke Park, Dublin
Donegal 1-12   Armagh 1-11

GAA Football All-Ireland Senior Championship Quarter-Final - Croke Park, Dublin
Dublin 2-22   Monaghan 0-11

1.

2.

(1) Armagh manager Paul Grimley leaves few in any doubt about his instructions
as he points in the direction of the Donegal goal late in their quarter-final. His
team spurn late chances and lose by just a point

(2) The bowl. All bar one of the Monaghan players retreat into their own half as
Eoghan O'Gara moves goalwards. A tenacious Monaghan rearguard display is
blown wide open by two Dublin goals in the run-up to the break

" They are an intelligent group of men and they kept probing the opposition and looking for gaps. They kept their composure and found small little chinks of light along the way **"**

Dublin manager Jim Gavin describes how his team broke down Monaghan's defence in the first half of their quarter-final

10   GAA Hurling All-Ireland Senior Championship Semi-Final - Croke Park, Dublin
Kilkenny 2-13   Limerick 0-17

17   GAA Hurling All-Ireland Senior Championship Semi-Final - Croke Park, Dublin
Tipperary 2-18   Cork 1-11

1.

2.

3

(1) It's all about timing and hand-eye co-ordination. Richie Power pulls off an exquisite piece of skill to direct a long high ball to the Limerick net as Kilkenny hold off a brave challenge from the Munster side

(2) Kilkenny manager Brian Cody is back where he wants to be – in an All-Ireland final - and it feels good

(3) Timber. James Barry makes his delivery and breaks the hurley of Paudie O'Sullivan in Tipperary's surprisingly comfortable win over Cork in their semi-final

❝ It was as hard as you could get. I thought Limerick played outstanding. They threw everything at us and we were tested in every way ❞

Kilkenny manager Brian Cody pays tribute to a heroic effort by the Shannonsiders

24 GAA Football All-Ireland Senior Championship Semi-Final - Croke Park, Dublin
Kerry 1-16   Mayo 1-16

30 GAA Football All-Ireland Senior Championship Semi-Final Replay - Gaelic Grounds, Limerick
Kerry 3-16   Mayo 3-13

(1) No winners in a draw. The reaction of Kerry defender Fionn Fitzgerald and Mayo manager James Horan says as much after the teams play out a riveting Croke Park draw. They will decamp to Limerick for the replay

(2) We've seen this before. Kerry forward Kieran Donaghy is renowned for his basketball skills but opts for samba soccer in this instance as Kerry steal a march on Mayo in their semi-final replay win at the Gaelic Grounds. Not before extra-time, mind you

1.

2.

" He was never a negative influence or a negative energy around the place. He was the opposite and he got that bit of karma he was looking for and that he deserved **"**

Kerry manager Éamonn Fitzmaurice delights in the 'rebirth' of forward Kieran Donaghy

1.

2.

❝ If we can clone 'Dolly the Sheep' it would be nice to clone Michael Murphy and have him in full-forward as well as around the middle of the park because of his leadership, intensity and honesty ❞

Jim McGuinness fantasises about an even more scientific approach to his style of football management

(1) Success tastes sweet, even at the semi-final stage. Donegal manager Jim McGuinness celebrates with kitman Joe McCloskey after the Ulster champions punch holes in Dublin's all-out attacking strategy and sensationally dethrone the reigning All-Ireland champions

(2) Tears all round. Alan Brogan and his son Jamie show their disappointment following the Donegal reversal. Many misread the picture, taken on a walk around the field, as a farewell but the long-serving Dub challenges that assumption the following day

SEPTEMBER '14

7 Electric Ireland GAA Hurling All-Ireland Minor Championship Final - Croke Park, Dublin
Kilkenny 2-17 Limerick 0-19

GAA Hurling All-Ireland Senior Championship Final - Croke Park, Dublin
Kilkenny 3-22 Tipperary 1-28

1.

2.

(1) The Nation's Playground on a day that matters so much to so many.
Croke Park on All-Ireland final day

(2) A treasure chest. Stadium announcer Jerry Grogan and Adam Burke
carry the Liam MacCarthy Cup in a box through the Croke Park service
tunnel on the day of the game

SEPTEMBER '14

7 Electric Ireland GAA Hurling All-Ireland Minor Championship Final - Croke Park, Dublin
Kilkenny 2-17   Limerick 0-19

1.

4.

(1) Autumn hurling and an idyllic sky setting. Clare goalkeeper Keith Hogan instructs his players to spread out before he delivers a puck-out following a Wexford point in the All-Ireland under-21 hurling final. The Banner conveyor belt continues to purr as they collect their third under-21 title on the trot

(2) The modern Clare hurler. The outstanding Tony Kelly, who typifies the recent resurgence in Clare hurling, raises the under-21 trophy in Thurles

(3) Happy or what? Cork camogie captain Anna Geary is a picture of elation as she lifts the O'Duffy Cup following their win over Kilkenny in the final

(4) The view is never the same from the losing camp. Time seems to stand still for Kilkenny's Shelly Farrell as she watches the celebrations

1.

2.

3.

4.

(1) All eyes on the ball. Kerry's Shane Ryan, Barry O'Sullivan, Robert Wharton, Andrew Barry, Mark O'Connor, Liam Carey, Micheál Burns and Matthew Flaherty watch a Donegal effort hit the Kerry upright in the closing stages of their All-Ireland minor final win

(2) The apples don't fall far from the tree. Killian Spillane, of the famous Kerry footballing dynasty, takes off against Ciarán Gillespie of Donegal

(3) The wait is over. Kerry captain Liam Kearney becomes the first All-Ireland minor-winning captain from the county in 20 years

(4) Going full circle. Former All-Ireland senior winning manager Jack O'Connor is back in the groove, this time as the successful manager of the minors

1.

2

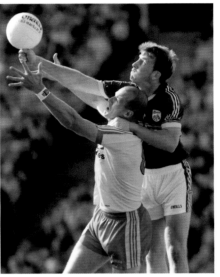

(1) The deck on the Starship Enterprise? It's 15 minutes before showtime on All-Ireland football final day and the Sunday Game editing team are in situ in the outside broadcast unit

(2) All-Ireland final starts don't get much better. Kerry forward Paul Geaney celebrates scoring a goal after just 50 seconds, striking low across Donegal goalkeeper Paul Durcan

(3) Jump start. Donnchadh Walsh uses Donegal midfielder Neil Gallagher as a platform as they compete for possession

1.

(1) Big men rising. Johnny Buckley and David Moran of Kerry contest a high ball with Donegal's Michael Murphy and Rory Kavanagh

(2) A tireless worker. Donegal's Rory Kavanagh embarks on another lung-bursting run as Kerry duo David Moran and Stephen O'Brien try to keep up with him

"It was an absolutely absorbing game of bad football"

RTÉ analyst Colm O'Rourke gives his view on the football final

1.

2.

3.

4.

(1) The seminal moment? Kieran Donaghy pounces to punish a mis-directed Donegal kick-out by goalkeeper Paul Durcan, and Kerry put daylight between the teams

(2) Playing to the gallery. Kieran Donaghy gestures to fans on Hill 16 following his crucial goal

(3) Strong forearm. Donegal's Leo McLoone attempts to dislodge the ball from David Moran's grasp

(4) Many sets of eyes but only one with the authority to alter proceedings. Kerry manager Éamonn Fitzmaurice patrols the line during the game

21   GAA Football All-Ireland Senior Championship Final - Croke Park, Dublin
Kerry 2-09   Donegal 0-12

1.

3.

(1) In such incidents are finals won and lost. Colm McFadden sees a late goal effort rebound off the Kerry post and, with it, goes Donegal's last hope

(2) A rueful glance. Donegal manager Jim McGuinness consoles Darach O'Connor after the defeat. Twelve days later McGuinness steps down from his role

(3) Pretty much what the GAA is about. Kerry midfielder David Moran celebrates with his parents Anne and the legendary Ógie, who knows this feeling well

(4) Double act. The Dr Crokes duo of Fionn Fitzgerald and Kieran O'Leary take a handle each to raise Sam skyward. It's Kerry's first title in five years

❝ I'm blessed and privileged to be part of the Kerry thing. That's 37 All-Ireland titles now. I'm minding this number 14 and someone else can have it next year. I'm going to be up in the terraces for the next 30 years looking down at other guys wearing it ❞

A reflective Kieran Donaghy after winning his fourth All-Ireland senior medal

1.

(1) Embracing the moment and each other. It wouldn't be All-Ireland final day without the winning team photo. Everyone wants in

(2) A selfie with a twist. Barry John Keane captures a special post-match shot in which he's the most prominent personality

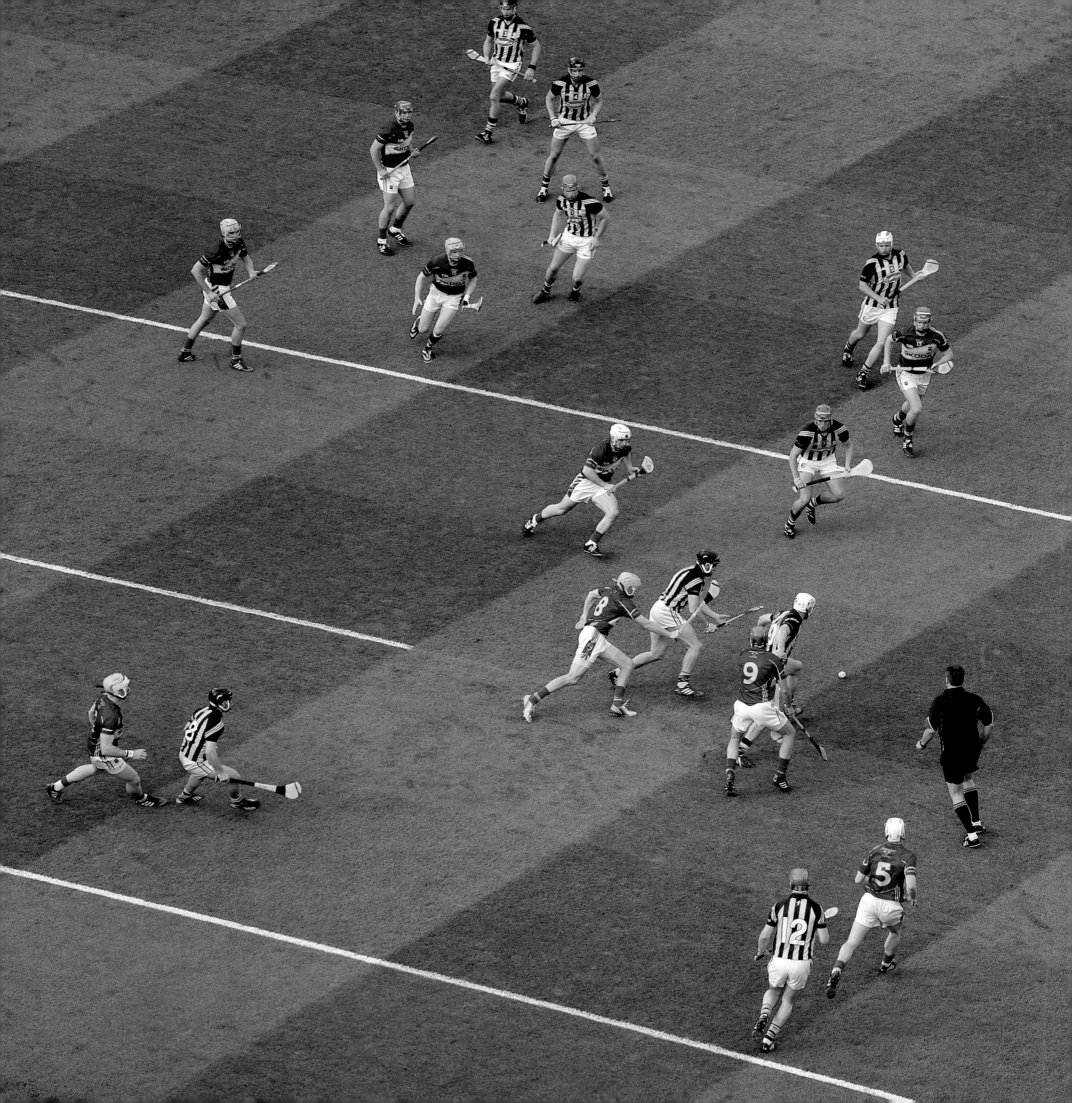

1.

2.

(1) The replay was unlikely to be as open as the drawn match, but it was intriguing nonetheless. The posse of players gathered around centrefield for the throw-in hints at what's about to unfold as time in possession comes at a premium on a day of superb defensive play

(2) Crowded out. Patrick Bonner, Tipperary's nonstop action man, attempts to burrow his way towards the Kilkenny goal but is blocked by goalkeeper Eoin Murphy, Pádraig Walsh, Kieran Joyce and JJ Delaney

1.

2.

(1) Vantage point. Henry Shefflin has the same view of the action as the spectators behind him, as another high ball is contested. Shefflin is about to enter the fray and earn his 10th All-Ireland medal on the field of play

(2) Simple yet crucial. Darren Gleeson makes two fine saves but the rebound from the second hangs up invitingly for John Power who is left with the easy task of tapping home. It's a score that tilts the pendulum Kilkenny's way

1.

2.

3.

" Kilkenny deserved the win. The game was played on their terms. When this game is played on someone's terms, they usually win and that is what happened today **"**

Tipperary manager Eamon O'Shea has no complaints as the Cats claim their 35th All-Ireland senior hurling title

4.

(1) Suck it up and come back bigger, better, stronger. Tipperary captain Brendan Maher consoles Pádraic Maher after the game

(2) A familiar pose. Kilkenny manager Brian Cody is not normally one to let emotion get the better of him but the seconds after the final whistle are an exception as he sees his team back on top of the pile again

(3) Rinneamar é. Lester Ryan accepts the Liam MacCarthy Cup and delivers an oration entirely in Irish. A fascinating Youtube clip released shortly after the final shows that he had practised giving a winning speech with some panache as a 10-year-old

(4) Henry Shefflin shares winning a 10th All-Ireland senior medal with his son Henry. It's impossible not to wonder…

2.

(1) Geraldine O'Flynn strikes beyond the despairing arms of Dublin's Leah Caffrey, left, and Sinéad Goldrick for what proves to be the winning point in the All-Ireland ladies football senior final

(2) This is what we do it all for. This incredible Cork team rejoice with manager Eamonn Ryan following an amazing comeback against Dublin to secure the Brendan Martin Cup for the ninth time in 10 years

GALLERY OF FANS